Together We Teach - Transforming Education Through Co-Teaching

Quick Reads for Busy Educators

Cheryl Angst

Published by Cheryl Angst, 2023.

TOGETHER WE TEACH - TRANSFORMING EDUCATION THROUGH CO-TEACHING

First edition. May 22, 2023.

Copyright © 2023 Cheryl Angst.

ISBN: 979-8223378327

Written by Cheryl Angst.

Also by Cheryl Angst

Quick Reads for Busy Educators

Gamifying Education - How to Engage and Motivate Students Through Games

Unlocking Gamification - Exploring the Impact and Importance in Education

Winning in the Classroom - Using Bartle's Gaming Styles to Empower Learners

Who Packed Your Parachute? Why Multiple Attempts on Assessments Matter

The Power of Discussion - A Guide to Using Literature Circles in the Classroom

Together We Teach - Transforming Education Through Co-Teaching

Mentoring 101 - Your Guide to Mentoring Student Teachers with Confidence

Table of Contents

Co-Teaching Promotes Inclusive Education

INCLUSIVE EDUCATION is a fundamental principle that aims to provide every student, regardless of their abilities or disabilities, with an equitable and quality education. It seeks to create an environment where all learners feel valued, respected, and supported in their academic and social growth. One powerful strategy that has emerged to support inclusive education is co-teaching. Co-teaching involves the collaboration of two or more educators, including general and special education teachers, working together in a shared classroom to meet the diverse needs of students. This book explores the power of co-teaching in promoting inclusive education and the numerous benefits it brings to both students and educators.

Creating an Inclusive Classroom Environment

Co-teaching fosters an inclusive classroom environment by promoting collaboration, acceptance, and diversity. Through shared responsibilities, co-teachers create a welcoming space where students of all abilities can learn and thrive together. By modeling respect and valuing each student's unique contributions, co-teaching sets the tone for inclusive practices and cultivates a sense of belonging.

Meeting Diverse Learning Needs

One of the key advantages of co-teaching is its ability to address diverse learning needs effectively. With two educators in the classroom, instructional strategies can be differentiated, allowing for individualized support and accommodations. Co-teachers can adapt lesson plans, materials, and teaching methods to cater to the varied strengths, learning styles, and challenges of students. This collaborative approach ensures that all students receive appropriate instruction and access to the curriculum.

Enhancing Student Engagement and Participation

Co-teaching promotes increased student engagement and participation. With multiple educators providing support and guidance, students are more likely to actively participate in classroom activities. Co-teachers can facilitate small group discussions, lead hands-on activities, and provide immediate feedback, fostering a dynamic learning environment that encourages student involvement. The collaborative nature of co-teaching also encourages peer-to-peer interaction, cooperative learning, and peer support, further enhancing student engagement and social development.

Supporting Social and Emotional Growth

Inclusive education not only focuses on academic achievement but also on social and emotional growth. Co-teaching provides opportunities for students to develop positive relationships and build social skills. With co-teachers modeling cooperation, empathy, and respect, students learn to value and appreciate individual differences. Additionally, the presence of two educators allows for more personalized attention and support, promoting positive behavior and emotional well-being among students.

Professional Collaboration and Growth

Co-teaching is not only beneficial for students but also for educators. Collaborating with a colleague allows teachers to pool their expertise, share resources, and exchange instructional strategies. Co-teaching creates an environment for professional growth, as educators learn from one another, observe different teaching styles, and expand their pedagogical knowledge. The ongoing collaboration and reflective practices in co-teaching contribute to the professional development of both general and special education teachers.

Benefits of Co-Teaching For Educators

CO-TEACHING HAS GAINED significant recognition in recent years due to its numerous benefits for both students and educators. In addition to the benefits of enhanced learning and academic achievement, increased student engagement and participation, and positive social interaction, noted in the previous section there two further benefits specific to teachers.

Professional Growth and Development

Co-teaching offers significant opportunities for professional growth and development for educators. Through collaboration, educators can share their expertise, exchange ideas, and learn from one another. Working together enables teachers to expand their instructional repertoire, discover new teaching strategies, and reflect on their own practices. Co-teaching also promotes a culture of continuous learning and improvement, as educators engage in collaborative planning, observation, and reflection. This professional growth ultimately benefits both the educators involved and the wider educational community.

Reduced Teacher Workload and Stress

Co-teaching can alleviate the workload and stress often experienced by educators. By sharing responsibilities, planning, and instructional delivery, educators can distribute the workload more effectively, allowing for greater efficiency and work-life balance. Co-teaching allows educators to tap into each other's strengths, expertise, and experiences, leading to a more streamlined and effective instructional process. Additionally, the support and collaboration between educators provide a valuable network for sharing ideas, problem-solving, and finding emotional support in the demanding field of education.

Chapter 1: Understanding Co-Teaching

WHEN I WAS FIRST ASSIGNED a co-teaching position, I have to admit that I didn't know much about what it entailed. I had been teaching for several years and had grown accustomed to running my classroom independently. So, when I learned that I would be sharing my classroom with another teacher, I was hesitant and not exactly thrilled about the idea.

As the start of the school year approached, I found myself feeling uncertain and anxious. I wondered how I would manage to work effectively with another teacher, share responsibilities, and ensure that our teaching styles aligned. I had concerns about losing control of my classroom and compromising my ability to meet the needs of my students. It felt like a daunting challenge that I wasn't sure I was ready for.

However, as the school year progressed, I started to see the benefits of co-teaching and began to appreciate the value it brought to my classroom. I realized that my co-teacher, who had a wealth of experience and expertise, could offer a fresh perspective and bring new ideas to the table. Our collaboration allowed us to combine our strengths, knowledge, and resources, resulting in enhanced instructional practices and increased support for our students.

One of the most significant advantages of co-teaching was the ability to differentiate instruction more effectively. With two teachers in the classroom, we were able to provide targeted support to students at different learning levels. While one of us worked with a small group, the other could provide individualized attention to students who needed it. This personalized approach allowed us to better meet the diverse needs of our students and ensure that no one was left behind.

Co-teaching also fostered a sense of community and inclusivity within our classroom. By modeling collaboration and teamwork, we encouraged our students to work together, respect different perspectives, and appreciate the strengths and abilities of their peers. It created a positive and supportive classroom environment where every student felt valued and included.

Over time, I realized that co-teaching wasn't about losing control or compromising my teaching style. It was about building a collaborative partnership that ultimately benefited our students. By pooling our expertise, we were able to create richer, more engaging learning experiences that addressed a wider range of student needs. It also alleviated some of the workload and allowed us to share the responsibilities of planning, grading, and managing the classroom effectively.

The Purpose of Co-Teaching

THE CO-TEACHING MODEL creates an inclusive classroom environment where diverse learners can thrive and reach their full potential.

Defining Co-Teaching

Co-teaching is a collaborative instructional approach in which two or more educators with complementary skills and expertise work together to deliver instruction to a diverse group of students. It involves a partnership where educators share responsibility for planning lessons, delivering content, and assessing student learning. Co-teachers collaborate closely to ensure that instruction is differentiated, inclusive, and tailored to meet the diverse needs of all learners in the classroom.

The Purpose of Co-Teaching

The purpose of co-teaching is multifaceted, with the overarching goal of creating an inclusive educational environment that supports the success of all students. Let's explore some of the key purposes and benefits of co-teaching:

- **Meeting Diverse Learner Needs:** Co-teaching allows for differentiated instruction, ensuring that all students, regardless of their abilities, learning styles, or cultural backgrounds, receive the support they need to succeed. By leveraging the expertise and skills of multiple educators, co-teaching enables instructional strategies to be tailored to individual student needs, promoting greater engagement and academic achievement.

- **Promoting Inclusion and Equity:** Co-teaching fosters an inclusive classroom culture that values and respects the diverse strengths and contributions of each student. Through collaborative planning and instruction, co-teachers can create learning experiences that honor students' identities, backgrounds, and learning preferences. This approach promotes equitable access to educational opportunities, reduces barriers to learning, and supports the social-emotional well-being of all learners.

- **Enhancing Instructional Effectiveness:** Co-teaching capitalizes on the strengths and expertise of each educator, resulting in enhanced instructional effectiveness. By combining their knowledge and skills, co-teachers can offer a broader range of instructional strategies, resources, and perspectives. This collaborative effort promotes creativity, innovation, and continuous improvement in instruction, leading to increased student engagement and deeper learning.

- **Supporting Professional Growth:** Co-teaching provides educators with opportunities for professional growth and development. Through collaborative planning and reflection, co-teachers can exchange ideas, share best practices, and learn from one another's experiences. This collaborative professional learning environment enhances teachers' pedagogical knowledge, expands their instructional repertoire, and cultivates a culture of continuous improvement.

- **Building Stronger Teacher-Student Relationships:** Co-teaching allows for more individualized attention and support for students. With multiple educators in the classroom, students have increased opportunities for personalized feedback, guidance, and mentoring. Co-teachers can build strong relationships with students, fostering a sense of belonging, trust, and support that positively impacts their academic and socio-emotional development.

Models and Approaches to Co-Teaching

THERE IS NO "ONE WAY" to co-teach. Below are various models and approaches to co-teaching, each highlighting their unique characteristics, benefits, and considerations. These models and approaches serve as valuable frameworks for educators seeking to implement effective co-teaching practices in their inclusive classrooms.

One Teach, One Observe

In this co-teaching model, one teacher assumes the role of the primary instructor while the other observes and gathers data on student performance, engagement, and instructional strategies. The observing teacher provides valuable feedback to improve instruction and student learning. This model allows for focused data collection, instructional reflection, and targeted interventions to meet student needs.

One Teach, One Assist

In the One Teach, One Assist model, one teacher takes the lead in delivering instruction, while the other provides support and assistance to individual students or small groups. The assisting teacher circulates the classroom, checking for understanding, offering additional explanations, and providing personalized support as needed. This approach ensures that all students receive appropriate attention and guidance during the lesson.

Parallel Teaching

In the Parallel Teaching model, the class is divided into two smaller groups, and each co-teacher delivers the same content simultaneously to their respective group. This approach allows for increased student engagement and participation, as well as more individualized instruction. It is particularly effective when differentiating instruction based on student needs, preferences, or learning styles.

Station Teaching

Station Teaching involves dividing the class into small groups and rotating through different instructional stations, each facilitated by a co-teacher. Each station offers a unique learning experience, such as independent practice, small-group discussion, or hands-on activities. Students have the opportunity to engage in diverse instructional strategies, receive targeted support, and collaborate with peers.

Team Teaching

Team Teaching, often considered the most intensive form of co-teaching, involves both educators actively sharing instruction, responsibilities, and classroom management. Co-teachers collaboratively plan, deliver, and assess lessons, ensuring seamless integration of their expertise and instructional approaches. This model promotes increased engagement, student participation, and diverse perspectives in the classroom.

Alternative Teaching

In the Alternative Teaching model, one teacher provides instruction to the larger group while the other works with a smaller group or individual students who require additional support or enrichment. This approach allows for targeted interventions and individualized instruction, ensuring that all students' unique needs are met.

In most co-teaching situations, the teachers move between these models throughout each day or, sometimes, within the same lesson. It should never be assumed that one teacher is always in a supporting role to the other. The benefit of co-teaching is each teacher brings their strengths to the shared classroom and both teachers should share in the leadership and support roles.

Considerations for Co-Teaching

While these models and approaches provide valuable frameworks for co-teaching, it is important to consider the following factors for successful implementation:

- **Clear Roles and Communication:** Co-teachers must establish clear roles and responsibilities, ensuring effective communication and coordination. Frequent and open communication promotes collaborative planning, instructional alignment, and consistent support for students.

- **Shared Planning Time:** Co-teachers should have dedicated planning time to collaboratively design instruction, set goals, create materials, and assess student progress. This shared planning time fosters a deeper understanding of student needs, effective differentiation, and cohesive instructional delivery.

- **Building Trust and Rapport:** Building trust and establishing positive professional relationships between co-teachers is essential. This foundation of trust allows for open dialogue, shared decision-making, and mutual support, creating a conducive environment for effective co-teaching.

Implementing co-teaching requires careful planning, clear communication, and ongoing professional development. When implemented effectively, co-teaching can transform educational experiences, empower students, and create inclusive learning environments that set the stage for academic success and personal growth.

Roles and Responsibilities

BY UNDERSTANDING AND embracing the roles and responsibilities that come with sharing a classroom, co-teachers can create a harmonious and effective learning environment that supports the diverse needs of all students.

Instructional Planning and Preparation

Co-teachers engage in collaborative instructional planning and preparation to ensure that lessons are aligned with curriculum standards, student goals, and individual needs. This involves jointly identifying learning objectives, selecting appropriate instructional strategies, and designing meaningful and engaging activities. Co-teachers share their expertise, knowledge, and experiences to create a cohesive and inclusive instructional plan.

Differentiation and Individualized Instruction

One of the primary responsibilities of co-teachers is to differentiate instruction to meet the diverse needs of learners. They collaboratively analyze student data, identify individual strengths and challenges, and develop strategies to address those needs. By providing individualized support, accommodations, and modifications, co-teachers ensure that all students have equitable access to the curriculum and can achieve their full potential.

Instructional Delivery and Classroom Management

During instruction, co-teachers share the responsibility of delivering lessons, providing explanations, modeling skills, and facilitating student engagement. They employ various instructional strategies, such as whole-group instruction, small-group work, or individualized instruction, based on the needs of the students. Co-teachers also work together to manage classroom behavior, establish routines, and create a positive and inclusive learning environment.

Assessment and Progress Monitoring

Co-teachers collaborate on the assessment and progress monitoring of students' learning. They jointly design formative and summative assessments, analyze data, and make instructional decisions based on student performance. Co-teachers communicate regularly to evaluate student progress, identify areas for improvement, and celebrate student achievements. By working together, they ensure that assessment practices are fair, valid, and provide meaningful feedback to students.

Collaboration and Communication

Effective collaboration and communication are vital in co-teaching partnerships. Co-teachers engage in ongoing dialogue, reflecting on instructional practices, sharing ideas, and problem-solving together. They establish open lines of communication with each other, students, parents, and other professionals involved in the students' education. Collaborative relationships built on trust and respect foster a positive and supportive learning community.

Chapter 2: Building a Strong Co-Teaching Partnership

IN THE REALM OF EDUCATION, collaboration is a powerful force that can bring about significant positive change. I had the privilege of witnessing the transformative power of collaboration when two experienced colleagues, Lisa and Sarah, made the decision to co-teach to better support the diverse needs of their students. The experience not only strengthened their teaching practices but also deepened their professional relationship.

Lisa and Sarah had been teaching in neighboring classrooms for several years. They both had extensive experience and a deep passion for education. Over time, they developed a close friendship, often discussing their teaching strategies, sharing resources, and seeking advice from one another. As they observed the increasing diversity in their classrooms, they recognized the need for a more inclusive and differentiated approach to instruction.

Driven by a shared commitment to meet the diverse needs of their students, Lisa and Sarah embarked on a co-teaching journey. They decided to combine their expertise, knowledge, and resources to create a collaborative classroom environment that would benefit all their students. They believed that their combined strengths and different perspectives would allow them to develop more effective instructional practices and provide the necessary support to all learners.

To begin, Lisa and Sarah engaged in thorough planning and preparation. They conducted in-depth discussions to identify the individual strengths and needs of their students. They collaborated on designing lessons that incorporated different teaching strategies, instructional materials, and assessment methods to accommodate a wide range of learning styles and abilities.

Throughout the co-teaching process, Lisa and Sarah engaged in ongoing communication and reflection. They regularly met to discuss lesson outcomes, student progress, and any challenges they encountered. They shared their observations, successes, and concerns, seeking solutions together. This open and honest dialogue not only improved their instructional practices but also deepened their professional relationship.

The impact of their co-teaching partnership on their students was profound. The diverse needs of the students were met more effectively, and the learning environment became more inclusive and supportive. Students experienced the benefits of two experienced teachers working in harmony, receiving personalized attention, and accessing a variety of instructional approaches. The classroom became a place where all students felt valued, challenged, and inspired to reach their full potential.

In retrospect, Lisa and Sarah's decision to embark on a co-teaching journey was an incredible turning point in their careers. Through their collaboration, they discovered the transformative power of working together. Their experience not only improved their instructional practices but also fostered a strong and lasting partnership. They recognized the immense value of collaboration and understood that by joining forces, they could have a profound impact on the lives of their students.

Trust and Open Communication

ONE OF THE KEY FACTORS that contribute to the success of co-teaching is the establishment of trust and open communication between co-teachers. Here we explore the importance of trust and communication in co-teaching, and provide strategies for building and maintaining strong collaborative partnerships.

Recognizing the Importance of Trust

Trust forms the foundation of any successful collaboration. In co-teaching, trust allows co-teachers to rely on each other's expertise, respect each other's ideas, and feel confident in sharing responsibilities. Trust creates a safe and supportive environment where co-teachers can take risks, experiment with instructional strategies, and learn from each other's strengths.

Establishing Clear Roles and Expectations

To foster trust, it is essential for co-teachers to establish clear roles and expectations from the beginning. Each co-teacher brings unique skills and knowledge to the partnership, and clearly defining these roles ensures that responsibilities are distributed equitably. Openly discussing and documenting these roles helps to avoid misunderstandings and promotes a sense of ownership and accountability.

Effective Communication Strategies

Open and frequent communication is crucial in co-teaching. Co-teachers should establish regular meeting times to discuss lesson planning, instructional strategies, student progress, and any concerns or challenges that arise. Active listening, sharing ideas, and providing constructive feedback are essential components of effective communication. Co-teachers should also establish protocols for resolving conflicts and addressing disagreements in a respectful and professional manner.

Building Positive Relationships

Building positive relationships between co-teachers is essential for fostering trust and open communication. Take the time to get to know each other, share personal experiences, and find common ground. Building rapport and a sense of camaraderie promotes a supportive and collaborative working environment.

Embracing Flexibility and Adaptability

Co-teachers must be flexible and adaptable in their approach to teaching. Recognize that each co-teacher may have different teaching styles, preferences, and perspectives. Embrace these differences and find ways to integrate them into the co-teaching partnership. Being open to new ideas and willing to adjust instructional strategies based on student needs fosters trust and shows a commitment to collaboration.

Reflecting and Evaluating the Partnership

Regular reflection and evaluation of the co-teaching partnership are essential to ensure ongoing growth and improvement. Co-teachers should regularly discuss their experiences, successes, challenges, and areas for growth. Reflecting together allows for adjustments and refinement of instructional practices, leading to a more effective and cohesive co-teaching partnership.

Collaborative Planning and Shared Decision-Making

COLLABORATIVE PLANNING and shared decision-making are vital components of successful co-teaching partnerships. When co-teachers come together to plan instruction and make decisions collectively, they tap into the diverse expertise and perspectives of each team member, leading to more effective and inclusive teaching practices

Maximizing the Benefits of Collaborative Planning

Collaborative planning allows co-teachers to pool their knowledge, skills, and experiences to create cohesive and comprehensive instructional plans. By engaging in joint lesson planning, co-teachers can integrate their respective strengths, knowledge of content, and expertise in pedagogy to develop engaging and differentiated lessons that meet the diverse needs of all students. Collaborative planning also fosters creativity, innovation, and shared ownership of the instructional process.

Establishing Clear Goals and Objectives

During collaborative planning, co-teachers should establish clear goals and objectives for their instruction. Together, they can define learning outcomes, identify essential skills and concepts, and align instruction with curriculum standards. By setting shared goals, co-teachers ensure that their teaching practices are focused and purposeful, leading to more meaningful and targeted learning experiences for students.

Leveraging Different Perspectives and Expertise

One of the greatest strengths of collaborative planning is the opportunity to leverage different perspectives and expertise. Each co-teacher brings unique skills, knowledge, and experiences to the partnership. By actively listening and valuing each other's contributions, co-teachers can tap into a broader range of instructional strategies, resources, and perspectives. This collaboration enriches the learning environment and provides students with a variety of approaches to understanding content.

Promoting Equity and Inclusion

Collaborative planning promotes equity and inclusion by ensuring that the needs of all students are considered. Co-teachers can collaborate to design instruction that addresses the diverse learning styles, abilities, and backgrounds of students. By incorporating differentiation strategies, accommodations, and modifications into their plans, co-teachers can create an inclusive learning environment where every student has the opportunity to succeed.

Shared Decision-Making for Effective Classroom Management

Shared decision-making in co-teaching extends beyond instructional planning to classroom management. Co-teachers should jointly establish rules, routines, and procedures that promote a positive and structured learning environment. By involving all team members in decision-making processes, co-teachers ensure consistency and a unified approach to behavior management, fostering a sense of ownership and responsibility among students.

Reflecting and Refining Instructional Practices

Collaborative planning and shared decision-making require ongoing reflection and evaluation. Co-teachers should regularly reflect on their instructional practices, assess student learning outcomes, and seek feedback from each other. By engaging in reflective conversations and analyzing student data, co-teachers can identify areas of success, challenges, and areas for improvement. This reflective practice allows for ongoing refinement of instructional strategies, leading to continuous growth and enhanced teaching practices.

Leveraging Strengths and Expertise

WHEN TEACHERS COLLABORATE and leverage their individual strengths, they create a dynamic learning environment that benefits all students.

Identifying and Valuing Individual Strengths

The first step in leveraging each teacher's strengths is to identify and value the unique skills and expertise that each co-teacher brings to the partnership. By recognizing and acknowledging these strengths, co-teachers can build a foundation of trust and respect, creating a positive collaborative environment. This process involves open and honest communication, where each teacher has the opportunity to share their areas of expertise and passion for specific subjects or instructional strategies.

Designating Roles and Responsibilities

Once the strengths of each co-teacher are identified, it is essential to assign roles and responsibilities that align with their expertise. By capitalizing on each teacher's strengths, the instructional workload can be effectively distributed, ensuring that both educators contribute meaningfully to the learning process. For example, one teacher may excel in content knowledge while the other may possess strong classroom management skills. By assigning responsibilities accordingly, co-teachers create a balanced and complementary instructional team.

Collaborative Lesson Planning and Instruction

Co-teachers should engage in collaborative lesson planning to integrate their strengths and expertise into the instructional process. By jointly designing lessons, they can combine their knowledge of content, instructional strategies, and student needs to create engaging and differentiated learning experiences. For instance, one teacher may excel in using technology to enhance instruction, while the other may have expertise in incorporating hands-on activities. By blending these strengths, co-teachers can create well-rounded and engaging lessons that cater to diverse learning styles and abilities.

Specialized Support and Differentiation

Each co-teacher may bring unique skills and experiences that can benefit specific groups of students. For example, one teacher may have expertise in working with students with special needs or English language learners. By leveraging these specialized skills, co-teachers can provide targeted support and differentiation to meet the specific needs of these students. This collaboration ensures that all learners receive the necessary support and access to the curriculum, fostering an inclusive and supportive learning environment.

Professional Learning and Growth

Leveraging each teacher's strengths and expertise in co-teaching not only benefits students but also promotes professional learning and growth for both educators. By working collaboratively and sharing knowledge, co-teachers have the opportunity to expand their instructional repertoire and learn from each other's experiences. This professional development enhances their teaching practice and deepens their understanding of effective instructional strategies, ultimately benefiting the entire school community.

Continuous Reflection and Feedback

To maximize the impact of leveraging strengths and expertise, co-teachers should engage in continuous reflection and feedback. Regular discussions and self-reflection allow educators to assess the effectiveness of their instructional strategies and identify areas for improvement. Providing constructive feedback to each other fosters growth and ensures that each teacher's expertise is continuously honed and refined.

Chapter 3: Creating an Inclusive Classroom Environment

AS A TEACHER IN A CO-teaching situation, I initially wondered how different it would be from running my own classroom. I had always strived to create an inclusive environment where every student felt valued and supported. However, I soon discovered that co-teaching not only reinforced my existing practices but also amplified them, making our classroom even more inclusive and powerful.

From the start, my co-teacher and I shared a common vision of creating an inclusive classroom environment. We believed in fostering a sense of belonging and providing equitable opportunities for all students to succeed.

We knew that collaboration and open communication were key to achieving our goals.

Together, we established a positive and welcoming classroom culture. We designed activities and classroom routines that encouraged student participation and engagement. We arranged flexible seating to accommodate different learning styles and preferences. We created a classroom community that embraced diversity, where students felt safe to express themselves and share their perspectives.

In our inclusive classroom, we recognized the importance of fostering positive relationships among students. We implemented cooperative learning strategies, encouraging students to work in teams and value each other's contributions. We facilitated discussions and activities that promoted empathy, understanding, and appreciation for diverse perspectives. Through class meetings and restorative practices, we resolved conflicts and nurtured a supportive community.

Reflecting on our co-teaching experience, I realized that while many of the inclusive practices were similar to what I had implemented in my own classroom, the presence of a teaching partner who shared the same vision made them even more powerful. We provided each other with support, encouragement, and different perspectives. Our collaboration allowed us to tackle challenges more effectively, share the workload, and brainstorm creative solutions.

The impact of our co-teaching on student learning and growth was remarkable. Students thrived in the inclusive environment we created together. They developed a stronger sense of belonging, gained a deeper understanding of diverse cultures and perspectives, and developed crucial social and emotional skills.

Fostering a Positive Classroom Climate

CREATING A POSITIVE and welcoming classroom climate is essential for effective co-teaching. When co-teachers establish a supportive and inclusive environment, students feel valued, engaged, and motivated to learn. Below are some strategies for fostering a positive and welcoming classroom climate when co-teaching.

Building Relationships and Collaboration

Building strong relationships between co-teachers and students is fundamental to creating a positive classroom climate. Co-teachers should take the time to get to know their students individually, showing genuine interest and care for their well-being. By establishing trust and rapport, co-teachers can create an atmosphere of mutual respect and understanding. Collaborative activities, such as ice-breakers, team-building exercises, or cooperative learning tasks, can further strengthen relationships among students and between co-teachers and students.

Setting Clear Expectations and Classroom Norms

Clear expectations and classroom norms provide a framework for behavior and create a positive and orderly learning environment. Co-teachers should collaborate to establish and communicate these expectations to students consistently. This includes guidelines for active participation, respectful communication, and responsible behavior. By setting clear boundaries, co-teachers create a sense of structure and safety, which allows students to focus on their learning and feel secure in the classroom.

Promoting Inclusivity and Celebrating Diversity

Inclusive practices are at the core of fostering a positive and welcoming classroom climate. Co-teachers should embrace and celebrate the diversity of their students, valuing each student's unique background, abilities, and perspectives. They can incorporate diverse materials, literature, and resources that reflect the experiences of all students. It is essential to create an environment where all students feel accepted, respected, and represented, fostering a sense of belonging for everyone.

Encouraging Active Participation and Collaboration

Co-teachers should create opportunities for active student participation and collaboration. By incorporating cooperative learning strategies, group projects, and discussions, co-teachers promote engagement and foster a sense of ownership in the learning process. Students should feel empowered to contribute their ideas, ask questions, and participate in class activities. Creating a safe space for students to express their thoughts and opinions promotes a positive classroom climate where everyone's voice is valued.

Providing Emotional Support and Encouragement

Emotional support plays a crucial role in fostering a positive classroom climate. Co-teachers should be attentive to students' social and emotional well-being, offering encouragement, empathy, and guidance. By creating a supportive environment, co-teachers can help students navigate challenges and build resilience. They should be available to listen, provide feedback, and offer appropriate support when needed.

Modeling Positive Behavior and Attitudes

Co-teachers serve as role models for students, and their behaviors and attitudes significantly influence the classroom climate. By demonstrating respect, kindness, and professionalism, co-teachers create a positive atmosphere that students can emulate. They should actively listen to students, value their contributions, and provide constructive feedback.

Modeling positive behavior sets a standard for student interactions and fosters a culture of mutual respect and support.

Student Engagement and Participation

CO-TEACHING PROVIDES a unique opportunity to promote student engagement and participation through a wide variety of strategies and practices.

Differentiated Instruction

Co-teaching allows educators to differentiate instruction to meet the diverse needs of students. By collaborating and sharing responsibilities, teachers can tailor their teaching strategies, materials, and approaches to accommodate individual learning styles, abilities, and interests. This approach ensures that all students are actively engaged and challenged at their appropriate level, promoting a sense of ownership and participation in the learning process.

Small Group and Individualized Instruction

Co-teachers can divide the class into smaller groups or work with individual students to provide targeted instruction and support. This approach enables teachers to address specific needs, offer personalized feedback, and foster meaningful interactions with students. Small group discussions, guided reading sessions, or one-on-one conferences allow for more focused engagement and participation, enhancing students' understanding and involvement in the learning activities.

Collaborative Learning Activities

Co-teaching provides an ideal environment for collaborative learning activities that encourage active participation and engagement. Teachers can design and facilitate group projects, problem-solving tasks, debates, or interactive discussions that require students to work together and actively contribute their ideas and perspectives. These activities promote critical thinking, communication, and teamwork skills while fostering a sense of shared responsibility for learning.

Varied Instructional Strategies

With two teachers in the classroom, co-teaching offers the opportunity to employ a wide range of instructional strategies to cater to different learning preferences and engage students effectively. Teachers can utilize hands-on experiments, multimedia presentations, technology tools, and real-world connections to make the learning experience more interactive and relatable. By employing diverse instructional methods, co-teaching keeps students engaged, motivated, and actively participating in the learning process.

Utilizing Peer-to-Peer Interactions

Co-teachers can encourage peer-to-peer interactions and collaborative learning among students. By facilitating structured discussions, cooperative learning tasks, and group projects, students learn from and support each other's learning. This fosters a sense of community, promotes active participation, and enhances understanding through peer explanations and shared perspectives. Peer interactions also help build social skills and create a positive and inclusive classroom environment.

Continuous Feedback and Assessment

Co-teachers can provide ongoing feedback and assessment to support student engagement and participation. By regularly monitoring student progress and understanding, teachers can identify areas of strength and areas that may require additional support. Timely feedback helps students stay on track, make adjustments, and feel supported in their learning journey. Co-teachers can collaborate on assessing student work, providing constructive feedback, and offering guidance for improvement, ultimately promoting active engagement and growth.

Differentiation and Individualized Support

IN CO-TAUGHT CLASSROOMS, differentiation and individualized support are key strategies for meeting the diverse needs of students. This section explores the significance of differentiation and individualized support in co-taught classrooms and highlights effective strategies for implementation.

Understanding Student Needs

Co-teachers begin by gaining a deep understanding of their students' strengths, challenges, and learning profiles. Through ongoing assessments, observations, and collaboration, they gather valuable information about individual students' academic abilities, preferences, and social-emotional needs. This knowledge serves as the foundation for designing differentiated instruction and individualized support.

Flexible Grouping

Co-teachers use flexible grouping strategies to organize students based on their specific needs and learning goals. Students may be grouped homogeneously or heterogeneously, depending on the learning objectives and tasks. Flexible grouping allows for targeted instruction, collaborative learning opportunities, and individualized support. It also enables students to work with peers who may complement their abilities and provide support or challenge as needed.

Varied Instructional Strategies

Differentiation involves using a range of instructional strategies and materials to address diverse learning needs. Co-teachers employ various approaches such as visual aids, manipulatives, technology tools, graphic organizers, and multimodal resources to cater to different learning styles and preferences. They differentiate content, process, and product to ensure that students have multiple entry points and opportunities for demonstrating their understanding.

Individualized Supports

Co-teachers provide individualized support to students who require additional assistance or accommodations. This may involve differentiated assignments, modified tasks, scaffolded instruction, or personalized learning plans. Individualized supports may also include providing extra time, utilizing assistive technology, or offering small-group or one-on-one instruction. By tailoring instruction to meet individual needs, co-teachers empower students to access the curriculum and make meaningful progress.

Ongoing Assessment and Feedback

Co-teachers use formative and summative assessments to monitor student progress and provide timely feedback. They collect data on individual student performance, analyze it collaboratively, and use it to inform instructional decisions. This allows for continuous evaluation of student growth and helps co-teachers adjust instruction to better meet students' needs. Feedback is specific, constructive, and actionable, supporting students' ongoing learning and improvement.

Chapter 4: Effective Instructional Strategies in Co-Teaching

EARLY ON IN MY CAREER I had been intrigued by the concept of co-teaching, but I didn't quite know what to expect when I was assigned to a co-teaching partnership for the first time. I had heard about the benefits of collaboration and the potential for creating an inclusive classroom, but I couldn't fully grasp the transformative power of the experience until I dove in.

I was paired with an experienced co-teacher who had a wealth of knowledge and expertise in working with diverse learners. From the first day, I was amazed at the level of collaboration and the seamless integration of our teaching styles. We quickly established a strong rapport, open communication, and a shared vision for our classroom.

One of the most incredible aspects of co-teaching was witnessing the impact it had on our students. The variety of instructional approaches, strategies, and perspectives we brought to the table allowed us to meet the diverse needs of our students in a way that would have been challenging to achieve alone. Together, we designed differentiated lessons that catered to different learning styles, provided additional support for struggling students, and challenged advanced learners.

What struck me the most was the way students responded to the co-teaching dynamic. They saw us as a united front, working together to support their growth and success. They felt safe to ask for help, seek clarification, and express their individual strengths and challenges. The power of having two educators in the room created an environment where students felt valued and empowered to take ownership of their learning.

I learned valuable lessons about the power of collaboration and shared decision-making. I saw firsthand how co-teaching allowed us to leverage each other's strengths and expertise, making us more effective educators. It also provided a space for continuous professional growth and reflection. We constantly shared feedback, exchanged ideas, and challenged each other to try new strategies.

Co-teaching has not only transformed my teaching practice, but it has also influenced my perspective on the power of collaboration in education. It has shown me that by working together, we can create inclusive classrooms where every student thrives. The impact on student learning and growth is undeniable, and I am grateful for the opportunity to be part of such a powerful experience.

Co-Designing and Delivering Instruction

ONE OF THE KEY ELEMENTS that distinguishes co-teaching from other instructional models is the co-designing and delivering of instruction. This collaborative approach ensures that both teachers contribute their expertise and perspectives, resulting in enhanced instructional practices and improved student outcomes.

Building on Complementary Strengths

Co-teachers bring different strengths and areas of expertise to the partnership. By leveraging these strengths, they can create a rich and comprehensive learning experience for students. Co-teachers should engage in open and honest discussions to identify their individual strengths and align them with instructional goals. This collaborative process allows teachers to capitalize on their expertise, whether it's content knowledge, pedagogical skills, technology integration, or classroom management strategies.

Co-Planning and Lesson Design

Co-teachers collaborate in the planning and design of lessons, ensuring that instructional goals, standards, and student needs are addressed effectively. This process involves joint decision-making, brainstorming, and sharing of ideas. Co-teachers consider various instructional strategies, resources, and assessments to create engaging and meaningful learning experiences. They align their instructional approaches, identify differentiation strategies, and determine the roles and responsibilities of each teacher during instruction.

Co-Delivery of Instruction

During instruction, co-teachers work together to deliver lessons in a coordinated and seamless manner. They may adopt different instructional formats, such as parallel teaching, station teaching, or team teaching, based on the needs of the students and the nature of the content. Co-teachers actively engage in facilitating discussions, providing clarifications, monitoring student progress, and offering support. By sharing the instructional load, they can provide more individualized attention and ensure that all students are actively involved in the learning process.

Effective Communication and Reflection

Co-teachers engage in ongoing communication to assess the effectiveness of their instruction and make necessary adjustments. They reflect on their collaborative practices, seek feedback from each other, and discuss strategies for improvement. Regular communication helps them address any challenges, celebrate successes, and maintain a positive and productive working relationship. Co-teachers should establish a supportive and non-judgmental environment where they can openly discuss instructional practices and share constructive feedback.

Flexibility and Adaptability

Co-teaching requires flexibility and adaptability to meet the ever-changing needs of students. Co-teachers should be willing to adjust instructional strategies, pacing, and resources based on ongoing assessment data and student feedback. They may need to modify lesson plans or differentiate instruction in real-time to address individual student needs. By being responsive and flexible, co-teachers can ensure that instruction is personalized and meaningful for all students.

Differentiated and Small Group Instruction

DIFFERENTIATED INSTRUCTION and small group instruction are two powerful instructional approaches that are often implemented in co-taught classrooms to meet the diverse needs of students. These strategies recognize that students have varying abilities, learning styles, and interests, and aim to provide targeted instruction and support to maximize their learning potential.

Differentiated instruction is an approach that acknowledges that students learn in different ways and at different paces. It involves tailoring instruction to address individual student needs, interests, and readiness levels. By providing multiple pathways for learning, teachers can ensure that all students have opportunities to engage, understand, and demonstrate their understanding of the content.

In a co-taught classroom, differentiated instruction takes on even greater significance as co-teachers can leverage their expertise and resources to provide a wider range of instructional strategies and materials. Each co-teacher can bring unique perspectives and strengths to the table, enabling them to address the diverse needs of students more effectively.

One of the key elements of differentiated instruction is flexible grouping. Co-teachers can collaborate to create flexible groups based on student needs and interests. These groups can be formed based on readiness levels, learning styles, or specific learning goals. This allows for targeted instruction and personalized support within each small group.

Small group instruction is an instructional strategy where teachers work with a smaller group of students, typically ranging from three to six, to provide focused and individualized instruction. This approach allows for more intensive and personalized interaction between teachers and students, promoting deeper understanding and engagement.

In a co-taught classroom, small group instruction can be particularly beneficial as co-teachers can lead different small groups simultaneously, capitalizing on their expertise and interests. This ensures that each small group receives specialized instruction that aligns with their specific learning needs.

The benefits of differentiated instruction and small group instruction in co-taught classrooms are numerous. First and foremost, these approaches promote student engagement and active participation. By tailoring instruction to meet individual needs, students are more likely to feel motivated and empowered to take ownership of their learning.

Furthermore, differentiated instruction and small group instruction allow for targeted remediation and enrichment. Students who require additional support can receive focused instruction and scaffolding to help them grasp challenging concepts, while those who are ready for greater challenges can be provided with extension activities and more complex tasks.

Another advantage is the opportunity for peer collaboration and cooperative learning. In small groups, students have the chance to work together, exchange ideas, and learn from one another. This fosters a collaborative and supportive classroom environment, where students build their social and communication skills alongside their academic knowledge.

Implementing differentiated instruction and small group instruction in co-taught classrooms requires careful planning and collaboration between co-teachers. It is essential to have clear learning objectives, well-defined groupings, and a variety of instructional materials and activities to meet the diverse needs of students.

Regular communication and reflection between co-teachers are also crucial for assessing student progress, adjusting instruction as needed, and sharing best practices. Co-teachers can collaborate to identify students who may benefit from specific interventions or modifications and develop appropriate strategies to support their learning.

When co-teachers collaborate and implement differentiated instruction and small group instruction, they create a dynamic and inclusive learning environment where every student has the opportunity to reach their full potential.

Chapter 5: Addressing Challenges and Problem-Solving

CO-TEACHING CAN BE a transformative and rewarding experience, but it's not without its challenges. I once found myself in a particularly challenging co-teaching situation that tested my patience, communication skills, and ability to collaborate effectively. However, through perseverance and a shared commitment to our students, my co-teacher and I were able to overcome our initial difficulties and develop a strong and successful partnership.

At the beginning of the school year, I was paired with a co-teacher who had a completely different teaching style and approach than mine. Our conflicting teaching philosophies and communication styles made it difficult for us to find common ground. We often disagreed on instructional strategies, classroom management techniques, and even how to structure our lessons. It seemed like every decision turned into a battle of wills, and it was taking a toll on our professional relationship and the overall classroom atmosphere.

The tension between us affected our students as well. They sensed the discord and uncertainty, which impacted their engagement and ability to thrive in the classroom. It was disheartening to see the negative impact our struggles were having on their learning experience. We knew we had to find a way to overcome our differences and work together for the sake of our students.

Recognizing the need for change, we decided to have an open and honest conversation about our concerns and frustrations. We set aside time to discuss our teaching philosophies, expectations, and goals for the students. It was a challenging conversation, but it allowed us to gain a better understanding of each other's perspectives and find areas of common ground.

To move forward, we agreed to approach co-teaching as a true partnership. We established regular times to meet and plan together, ensuring that both of our voices were heard and respected. We identified our individual strengths and assigned responsibilities accordingly, leveraging each other's expertise to create a cohesive instructional plan. By playing to our strengths, we were able to capitalize on our unique talents and enhance our teaching practices.

Gradually, as we worked together more closely, our relationship began to transform. We started to appreciate each other's strengths and recognize the unique contributions we brought to the classroom. We developed a mutual respect and admiration for one another's teaching abilities. We became a true team, supporting each other, bouncing ideas off one another, and celebrating our successes together.

As our partnership grew stronger, we witnessed the positive impact on our students. They began to thrive in the classroom, benefiting from the combined expertise and differentiated instruction we provided. The classroom became a more inclusive and supportive environment where every student felt valued and empowered to succeed.

Looking back on that challenging co-teaching experience, I am grateful for the growth and learning it brought. It taught me the importance of open communication, flexibility, and a shared commitment to our students' success. It demonstrated the power of perseverance and the ability to overcome obstacles when working as a team.

Common Challenges in Co-Teaching

CO-TEACHING, WITH ITS collaborative and inclusive nature, offers numerous benefits for both students and educators. However, like any teaching approach, it comes with its own set of challenges.

Role Clarification

One of the key challenges in co-teaching is ensuring clear and defined roles for each co-teacher. It is essential to establish a shared understanding of responsibilities and expectations to avoid confusion and potential conflicts.

Strategies to Overcome This Challenge

- **Engage in Open and Honest Communication:** Have a candid conversation with your co-teacher(s) to clarify roles and responsibilities. Discuss individual strengths, expertise, and teaching preferences to find a balance that maximizes collaboration and supports student needs.

- **Collaboratively Plan and Reflect:** Regularly engage in collaborative planning sessions to discuss instructional strategies, content coverage, and classroom management. Reflect on what is working and what needs adjustment, making necessary modifications to optimize co-teaching effectiveness.

Time Management

Co-teaching requires effective time management to ensure smooth coordination and meaningful instruction. Balancing two or more professionals' schedules and responsibilities can be challenging, especially when planning, delivering instruction, and assessing student progress.

Strategies to Overcome This Challenge

- **Establish a Shared Planning Schedule:** Set aside dedicated time for collaborative planning and reflection. Create a consistent routine to align schedules and allow for regular communication and joint decision-making.

- **Divide Tasks and Responsibilities:** Delegate specific tasks and responsibilities between co-teachers to make the most efficient use of time. This may include dividing lesson preparation, grading, or classroom management duties based on individual strengths and expertise.

Classroom Management

Managing a diverse classroom with multiple teachers can present challenges in maintaining a positive and organized learning environment. Ensuring smooth transitions, addressing student behavior, and fostering a cohesive classroom culture require effective collaboration and communication.

Strategies to Overcome This Challenge

- **Develop a Shared Behavior Management Plan:** Collaboratively establish clear expectations and consequences for behavior. Consistency in approach and reinforcement across co-teachers helps students understand and follow the established guidelines.

- **Coordinate Transitions and Procedures:** Plan and rehearse transitions between activities to minimize disruptions. Ensure that procedures, such as collecting assignments or taking attendance, are clearly communicated and coordinated to maintain a structured and orderly classroom environment.

Communication and Collaboration

Effective communication and collaboration between co-teachers are crucial for successful co-teaching. Differences in teaching styles, approaches, or conflicting perspectives can hinder effective collaboration if not addressed.

Strategies to Overcome This Challenge

- **Foster Open and Respectful Communication:** Cultivate an environment of trust and mutual respect, where co-teachers feel comfortable expressing their ideas, concerns, and suggestions. Regularly schedule meetings to discuss instructional practices, share feedback, and address any issues or conflicts that may arise.

- **Reflect and Learn Together:** Engage in collaborative reflection to evaluate the effectiveness of co-teaching strategies and make adjustments as necessary. Use each other's strengths and expertise to learn and grow professionally, leveraging the power of collective wisdom.

Collaborative Problem-Solving and Conflict Resolution

WHILE CO-TEACHING CAN be a rewarding and effective instructional approach, it also requires strong communication skills and the ability to navigate conflicts and challenges that may arise. Collaborative problem-solving and conflict resolution strategies are essential tools for co-teachers to maintain a harmonious and productive working relationship.

Open and Honest Communication

Effective communication is the foundation of successful co-teaching. Co-teachers should establish an open and respectful line of communication from the start, creating an environment where concerns, ideas, and feedback can be freely shared. When conflicts or challenges arise, it is crucial to communicate openly and honestly to address the issues.

- **Active Listening:** Listen attentively to the perspectives and concerns of your co-teacher. Practice active listening by paraphrasing, asking clarifying questions, and demonstrating empathy.

- **Expressing Concerns Constructively:** When addressing a conflict or problem, use "I" statements to express how the situation makes you feel and focus on the specific behavior or issue at hand. Avoid blaming or making personal attacks.

- **Regular Check-Ins:** Schedule regular check-in meetings to discuss instructional strategies, student progress, and any concerns that may arise. This ongoing communication allows for early identification and resolution of issues.

Collaborative Problem-Solving

Co-teachers should approach challenges as opportunities for growth and improvement. Collaborative problem-solving involves working together to identify solutions, brainstorming ideas, and reaching consensus on the best course of action.

- **Define The Problem:** Clearly articulate the problem or challenge you are facing. Be specific and focus on the issue at hand.

- **Brainstorm Solutions:** Generate a variety of possible solutions to address the problem. Encourage creativity and open-mindedness during this process.

- **Evaluate Solutions:** Assess the pros and cons of each solution and consider their feasibility, effectiveness, and alignment with student needs.

- **Reach Consensus:** Engage in open discussion and negotiation to reach a consensus on the most viable solution. Each co-teacher should feel heard and valued during this process.

Seek Mediation if Needed

In some cases, conflicts or challenges may require external support to reach a resolution. Seeking mediation from a trusted colleague, instructional coach, or administrator can provide valuable insights and facilitate a constructive dialogue.

- **Neutral Mediator:** Engage a neutral party who can facilitate discussions between co-teachers, ensuring that all perspectives are heard and guiding the conversation towards a resolution.

- **Mediation Process:** During mediation, co-teachers should be encouraged to express their concerns, listen to each other's viewpoints, and work towards finding a mutually beneficial solution.

Reflect On, and Learn from, Conflict

Conflict can be an opportunity for growth and improvement. Co-teachers should engage in reflective practices to learn from conflicts and identify areas for professional development.

- **Self-Reflection:** Reflect on your own actions, behaviors, and contributions to the conflict. Consider how you could have approached the situation differently and what you can learn from the experience.

- **Collaborative Reflection:** Engage in joint reflection with your co-teacher(s) to analyze the conflict, its root causes, and potential strategies for prevention or resolution in the future.

Chapter 6: Building Partnerships with Others

AS A LEARNING SUPPORT teacher, I had the opportunity to provide in-class support in a co-taught classroom three blocks a week. At first, I wasn't sure what to expect or how my role would fit into the dynamic of the classroom. However, as time went on, I realized just how valuable my presence and support were for the students and the co-teachers.

One of the things I loved most about being part of a co-taught classroom was the collaborative atmosphere. The co-teachers and I worked closely together to plan lessons and activities that catered to the diverse needs of the students.

We shared ideas, resources, and strategies to ensure that all students had access to quality education.

During the three blocks that I was in the classroom, I had the opportunity to work with students in small groups or one-on-one. This allowed me to provide individualized support and address specific learning needs. Whether it was helping a student understand a math concept, providing extra practice for reading comprehension, or assisting with organization skills, I could tailor my instruction to meet each student's unique needs.

Working closely with the co-teachers allowed me to learn from their expertise and experience. We shared ideas on instructional strategies, behavior management techniques, and differentiation methods. This collaboration not only enhanced my own professional growth but also contributed to the collective success of the students.

Working alongside the co-teachers and witnessing the positive outcomes for the students reaffirmed my passion for inclusive education and the power of teamwork in meeting the diverse needs of learners.

Building Partnerships with Families

BUILDING STRONG PARTNERSHIPS with parents and families can have a significant impact on student success, classroom dynamics, and overall educational outcomes. In this section, we will explore the importance of building partnerships with parents and families when co-teaching and the benefits they bring to the learning community.

Shared Understanding and Support

Building partnerships with parents and families fosters a shared understanding of the co-teaching approach, classroom expectations, and instructional strategies. Effective communication and collaboration ensure that everyone is working towards common goals and supports a cohesive learning environment for students.

- **Regular Communication:** Establish open lines of communication with parents and families, providing them with updates on classroom activities, student progress, and upcoming events. This can be done through newsletters, emails, parent-teacher conferences, or online platforms.

- **Parent Education:** Offer workshops or information sessions specifically designed for parents and families to familiarize them with co-teaching principles, inclusive practices, and ways they can support their child's learning at home.

Individualized Support and Collaboration

Parents and families possess valuable insights into their child's strengths, interests, and learning styles. Collaborating with them allows for a more holistic understanding of the student and enables teachers to provide individualized support and accommodations that enhance their learning experience.

- **Family Input:** Seek input from parents and families regarding their child's unique needs, preferences, and learning goals. This input can inform instructional planning, differentiation strategies, and the selection of appropriate resources.

- **Home-School Partnerships:** Collaborate with parents and families to develop strategies that bridge the gap between home and school. This can include sharing resources, establishing consistent expectations, and creating opportunities for home-based learning activities.

Supportive Learning Environment

When parents and families are actively engaged in the co-teaching process, a supportive and inclusive learning environment is created. This sense of community and partnership contributes to students' overall well-being, motivation, and academic success.

- **Involvement in Classroom Activities:** Encourage parents and families to participate in classroom activities, special events, or volunteer opportunities. Their presence in the classroom not only supports student learning but also strengthens the sense of community.

- **Celebrating Student Achievements:** Recognize and celebrate student achievements together with parents and families. This can be done through awards ceremonies, showcases, or parent-teacher celebrations to highlight the progress and accomplishments of students.

- **Collaborative Problem-Solving:** Involve parents and families in collaborative problem-solving discussions, where challenges or barriers are identified, and solutions are explored together. This collaborative approach promotes a sense of shared responsibility and ownership in supporting student success.

Coordinating Support from Specialists

IN A CO-TEACHING ENVIRONMENT, collaboration goes beyond just the two teachers in the classroom. It extends to include specialists such as special education teachers, speech therapists, occupational therapists, and other professionals who provide additional services and support to students with diverse learning needs. Coordinating these services effectively is essential to ensure that all students receive the necessary support to thrive academically and socially.

Open and Transparent Communication

Effective coordination starts with open and transparent communication between co-teachers and specialists. Clear lines of communication ensure that everyone involved is well-informed and can work together towards common goals.

- **Regular Meetings:** Schedule regular meetings with specialists to discuss student needs, progress, and interventions. These meetings provide an opportunity to share insights, strategies, and progress updates.

- **Share Information:** Share relevant student information, Individualized Education Programs (IEPs), and any other assessments or documentation with specialists. This information will help them better understand the students' needs and provide targeted support.

Collaborative Planning and Goal Setting

Coordinating services requires collaborative planning and goal setting among co-teachers and specialists. By aligning their efforts, they can ensure that interventions and support are integrated seamlessly into the classroom environment.

- **Collaborative Planning Meetings:** Conduct joint planning sessions with specialists to discuss student goals, accommodations, and modifications. Determine how their services can be incorporated within the co-teaching framework to provide the most effective support.

- **Set Common Goals:** Establish shared goals for student progress and growth. This allows specialists to align their interventions and support strategies with the instructional goals of the co-teaching team.

Coordinated Instruction and Support

Co-teachers and specialists need to work together to ensure that instruction and support are coordinated and complementary. This collaboration helps to create a cohesive learning experience for all students.

- **Team Teaching:** Engage in team teaching, where co-teachers and specialists collaborate in delivering instruction. This can involve co-planning lessons, co-leading activities, or providing targeted interventions during classroom instruction.

- **Flexible Grouping:** Implement flexible grouping strategies that allow students to receive targeted support from specialists while maintaining their involvement in the co-teaching classroom. This may involve small group instruction or individualized interventions.

Regular Progress Monitoring and Feedback

Monitoring student progress is essential to determine the effectiveness of interventions and support services. Co-teachers and specialists should engage in regular progress monitoring and provide feedback to one another.

- **Data Sharing:** Share assessment data, progress reports, and observations between co-teachers and specialists. This data helps inform instructional decisions and allows for targeted interventions and adjustments as needed.

- **Collaborative Problem-Solving:** Engage in collaborative problem-solving discussions to address any challenges or concerns that may arise. Co-teachers and specialists can work together to develop strategies and modifications to support student progress.

Conclusion

AS A PRINCIPAL, I HAVE had the privilege of witnessing the transformative power of co-teaching in our school. Co-teaching has become a cornerstone of our inclusive education approach, fostering a collaborative and supportive environment that benefits both students and teachers alike.

From the moment we introduced co-teaching into our school, I observed a significant shift in the classroom dynamics and student outcomes. The collaboration between teachers created a seamless integration of expertise and instructional strategies, resulting in enhanced learning experiences for all students. The power of two teachers working together in the same classroom was evident in the increased engagement, participation, and achievement of our students.

Beyond the academic benefits, co-teaching fostered a sense of belonging and inclusion among our students. Students with special needs or those who required additional support felt valued and embraced as integral members of the classroom community. The presence of two teachers created a safe and supportive space where students felt comfortable seeking help and participating actively in their learning.

Co-teaching also had a profound impact on our teachers. The collaborative nature of co-teaching encouraged professional growth and development. Teachers had the opportunity to learn from each other, share best practices, and collaborate on instructional decisions. This collegial partnership elevated their teaching skills and expanded their repertoire of strategies, ultimately benefiting their individual classrooms and the entire school community.

The success of co-teaching in our school can be attributed to a shared vision of inclusive education and a commitment to collaboration. The dedication and passion of our teachers, combined with the support of our entire school community, have made co-teaching an integral part of our educational fabric.

The power of co-teaching in our school has been undeniable. It has transformed our classrooms into inclusive, dynamic, and engaging spaces where every student has the opportunity to thrive. The collaborative partnerships among teachers have not only improved student outcomes but also strengthened the professional growth and satisfaction of our educators. Co-teaching has truly become a driving force in creating a school culture that values and embraces the diverse needs and strengths of all learners.

Recap of the Key Principles and Strategies

———

THROUGHOUT THIS BOOK, we have explored various aspects of co-teaching, from its definition and purpose to the different models and strategies employed by co-teachers. Now, let's recap the key principles and strategies that contribute to successful co-teaching.

Shared Vision and Collaboration

Co-teachers should establish a shared vision for student success and actively collaborate to achieve it. This involves setting common goals, discussing instructional approaches, and aligning teaching practices. Collaboration lays the foundation for effective co-teaching partnerships.

Clear Roles and Responsibilities

Clarifying roles and responsibilities is essential in avoiding confusion and maximizing instructional efficiency. Co-teachers should clearly define their roles, such as lead teacher, support teacher, or content specialist, and ensure that each role complements the other.

Open Communication and Trust

Open communication fosters a positive co-teaching environment. Co-teachers should actively listen to each other, share ideas, concerns, and feedback, and maintain a respectful and trusting relationship. Regular communication helps address challenges and promotes continuous improvement.

Differentiation and Individualized Instruction

Co-teaching allows for greater differentiation and individualized instruction. Co-teachers should leverage their expertise to provide targeted support to students with diverse learning needs. This may involve modifying lessons, providing accommodations, or delivering small-group instruction.

Collaborative Planning and Co-Designing Instruction

Co-teachers should engage in collaborative planning to ensure instructional alignment and coherence. By co-designing lessons and activities, they can integrate their strengths and expertise, creating engaging and meaningful learning experiences for all students.

Flexibility and Adaptability

Co-teaching requires flexibility and adaptability to respond to the changing needs of students. Co-teachers should be open to adjusting instructional strategies, modifying plans, and making on-the-spot decisions to meet individual student needs.

Ongoing Reflection and Professional Growth

Reflection is key to continuous improvement in co-teaching. Co-teachers should regularly reflect on their practices, student outcomes, and the effectiveness of their collaboration. Engaging in professional development opportunities specific to co-teaching supports their growth and enhances their instructional skills.

Building Relationships with Students

Co-teachers should prioritize building positive relationships with students. This includes getting to know students' strengths, interests, and learning styles, and providing a supportive and inclusive classroom environment that values student voice and participation.

Utilizing Resources and Support

Co-teachers should take advantage of available resources and support. This may include collaborating with specialists, seeking guidance from instructional coaches or administrators, and accessing professional learning communities focused on co-teaching.

Empowering Educators to Embrace Co-Teaching

EDUCATION IS A TRANSFORMATIVE journey that shapes the minds and futures of our students. As educators, we have the incredible opportunity and responsibility to create inclusive classrooms that celebrate diversity and ensure every student's success. One powerful tool that can help us achieve this is co-teaching. Co-teaching, when embraced with enthusiasm and a commitment to collaboration, has the potential to revolutionize our classrooms and empower all students to reach their full potential.

One of the most significant benefits of co-teaching is its ability to provide individualized support to students with diverse learning needs. By pooling our expertise, we can differentiate instruction, modify materials, and implement targeted interventions to meet the unique needs of every student in our classroom. Through collaborative planning and co-designing of instruction, we can create engaging and inclusive lessons that cater to various learning styles, abilities, and interests. This approach not only enhances academic achievement but also promotes social-emotional development and self-confidence in our students.

Co-teaching also cultivates a culture of shared responsibility and open communication. By working together, we create a space where ideas are freely exchanged, feedback is constructively given and received, and challenges are collectively addressed. This collaboration helps us develop a deeper understanding of our students' strengths, challenges, and aspirations. It allows us to tap into each other's knowledge and experiences, ensuring that our instructional practices are responsive and effective.

As we embrace co-teaching, it is essential to foster a positive mindset and a willingness to learn from each other. We must recognize that collaboration is not about relinquishing control or diluting our expertise but rather about enhancing our instructional impact and promoting student success. By embracing co-teaching, we demonstrate our commitment to inclusivity, equity, and the belief that every student deserves the best education possible.

To fully harness the power of co-teaching, we must provide educators with the support, resources, and professional development they need. Administrators can play a crucial role in creating a culture that values and encourages co-teaching by providing dedicated time for collaboration, offering relevant training opportunities, and recognizing and celebrating the successes of co-teaching teams. By investing in the growth and empowerment of our educators, we pave the way for a more inclusive and equitable education system.

By embracing collaboration, celebrating diversity, and tapping into the collective expertise of our teaching colleagues, we can provide a truly transformative educational experience. Let us empower ourselves and our colleagues to embrace co-teaching as a driving force for inclusive education. Together, we can build a future where every student feels valued, supported, and empowered to achieve their dreams.

Further Reading

BENINGHOF, ANNE M. *Co-Teaching That Works: Structures and Strategies for Maximizing Student Learning*. Wiley, 2020.

Conderman, Greg, Bresnahan, Val, and Pedersen, Theresa. *Purposeful Co-Teaching: Real Cases and Effective Strategies*. SAGE Publications, 2008.

Fattig, Melinda L., and Taylor, Maureen Tormey. *Co-Teaching in the Differentiated Classroom: Successful Collaboration, Lesson Design, and Classroom Management*. Wiley, 2008.

Stein, Elizabeth. *Two Teachers in the Room: Strategies for Co-Teaching Success*. Routledge, 2017.

Don't miss out!

Visit the website below and you can sign up to receive emails whenever Cheryl Angst publishes a new book. There's no charge and no obligation.

https://books2read.com/r/B-A-SBAY-CJMJC

BOOKS 2 READ

Connecting independent readers to independent writers.

About the Author

Cheryl Angst has been teaching in the classroom for over twenty-five years. With a Masters in curriculum and instruction, her passion centers around finding tips, tricks, and strategies to enhance her practice.

Cheryl is a firm believer that learning should be fun for both the students and the teacher. If it isn't engaging, or doesn't spark joy, it's likely able to be done differently.

The "Quick Reads for Busy Educators" series is designed to maximize the precious time educators have. Each book is short enough to be read in an hour or less, but contains a wealth of information on the topic. Some books are overviews of strategies and approaches (enough to help educators decide if it's for them) and some are deeper dives into specific aspects of those larger approaches. This allows busy educators to grab the information they need quickly and efficiently.

If there's a topic you'd like to see covered in the "Quick Reads" series, please let us know!